Who Is Pelé?

Who Is Pelé?

by James Buckley Jr.

illustrated by Andrew Thomson

Penguin Workshop

To everyone who loves the "beautiful game"!—JB

For Rhia—AT

PENGUIN WORKSHOP
An Imprint of Penguin Random House LLC, New York

Text copyright © 2018 by James Buckley Jr. Illustrations copyright © 2018 by Penguin Random House LLC. All rights reserved. Published by Penguin Workshop, an imprint of Penguin Random House LLC, New York. PENGUIN and PENGUIN WORKSHOP are trademarks of Penguin Books Ltd. WHO HQ & Design is a registered trademark of Penguin Random House LLC. Printed in the USA.

Visit us online at www.penguinrandomhouse.com.

Library of Congress Control Number: 2018012956

ISBN 9780399542619 (paperback)   10 9
ISBN 9780399542626 (library binding)   10 9 8 7 6 5 4 3

Contents

Contents

Who Is Pelé?

In the summer of 1956, Pelé was homesick.

Pelé (say: PEH-lay) had arrived in the city of Santos, Brazil, just weeks earlier. He had grown up in Bauru, a tiny town to the west, but his incredible skills on the soccer field got him noticed by a team called Santos. He was only fifteen, and moving to the city had been a major decision for Pelé.

Without soccer, he might still be shining shoes or working in a field. Most of his friends on his hometown team could never dream of leaving Bauru. Now, on the Santos team, Pelé would earn enough money to support his family. And he could make his dream of becoming a soccer star come true.

At just over five feet tall, Pelé was small for

his age. He was an amazing player who could dribble well, and he was very quick. On his new team, though, he was playing against older, larger adults. He was worried he would not succeed. He was also living away from home for the first time.

And Santos was a strange place. Then he missed an easy penalty shot during a game that cost his team a victory. He was embarrassed and sad. Pelé had had enough of life in the big city. *That's it*, he thought, *I'm quitting*.

Early in the morning, he packed his bag and tiptoed out of his room. He had just enough money for a bus ticket back to Bauru. But as he walked quietly through the players' dormitory, he was stopped by a man who worked for the team. Big Sabu helped the players with their gear and watched over the young players. In his many years with Santos, he had seen other teens like Pelé. They were young, scared, and often thought of quitting. So Big Sabu stopped Pelé and told him he could not leave without permission. He wanted to keep Pelé on team Santos. Pelé listened and made an important decision. He headed back to his room. He would keep aiming for his dream.

And it turned out to be the right decision. Pelé had arrived at Santos as a very good player, but that was not enough. Pelé worked hard and soon learned to do more than just dribble. He worked on shooting and passing and being in the right position to help his teammates. He ate more, exercised, and grew stronger and more confident.

In a few months, he was one of the team's stars, scoring goal after goal. With Pelé's help, Santos became one of the top teams in the country. When Pelé was only seventeen, he was named to the national team for Brazil and helped his country win its first World Cup championship!

In the years that followed, Pelé became the best, and most famous, soccer player in the world. He helped Brazil win three World Cup titles and scored more than 1,200 goals for his teams and his country. He also traveled to the United States in 1975 and helped the sport of soccer become popular among Americans. As the best player in the world's favorite sport, Pelé became an ambassador for soccer and a symbol for the sport itself.

CHAPTER 1
The Boy Who Loved Soccer

Edson Arantes do Nascimento was born on October 23, 1940, in the tiny village of Três Corações (say: TRACE kor-ah-SOYS), Brazil. Even in 1940, there were many parts of the world that did not have electricity. Most of southeastern Brazil was one of those areas. In honor of their village finally getting electricity, Edson's parents named their first son after the American inventor Thomas Edison.

Edson's father was named João Ramos but went by the nickname Dondinho. Most Brazilian men are known by a nickname. He was a soccer player for the town's team. Edson's mother was named Celeste. Two years later, his mother had another son, Jair. Edson had not yet been nicknamed "Pelé."

Like all Brazilians, the Nascimento family spoke Portuguese. Brazil had been a colony of Portugal until 1822, when it gained independence. In the 1700s and 1800s, millions of Africans had been brought to Brazil as slaves to work for the

Portuguese. The Nascimento family had ancestors among those African people, so Edson had very dark skin.

Dondinho loved playing soccer and hoped that his sons would follow him. But playing professional soccer was not an easy life. In Brazil at this time, every village and town had a team. But only the very top players on the biggest teams earned the best salaries. The smaller teams, like the one in Três Corações and nearby towns, could not pay their players well. And that made life hard for Edson's family. They lived in a brick house that was nearly falling down in places.

And Edson didn't own a pair of shoes until he was seven years old.

In 1943, Edson's sister was born. She was named Maria Lúcia.

When Edson was four, Dondinho was asked to play for a team in Bauru, a larger town to the south. He was also promised a second job for when he was not playing soccer. This was good news for the family. On the way to Bauru, Edson was excited to ride a train for the first time. He was thrilled to see the country of Brazil rush by the open window. He nearly fell out of one before being caught by Dondinho!

Life in Bauru was not easy. The family's house was also very crowded. Edson's grandmother and his uncle Jorge had also moved to Bauru so the family could stay together. The house had only a small backyard, and it was often muddy. They had no air conditioning in the steamy summers. And they heated the house during the winters with a woodstove, which they also used for cooking. It was Edson's job to stack the wood  that was delivered to the house each week.

Dondinho's team did not provide the second job it had promised him. And he had injured his knee, which meant he could not play all the time. Sometimes the family struggled just to have enough to eat. Their relatives tried to help them out. Even Edson had to help. He worked as a shoeshine boy at the railroad station. He also sometimes worked at the soccer stadium when Dondinho played. He loved watching his tall, strong father leap above the other teams' players to knock the ball into the goal with his head.

Soccer or Football?

Around the world, the sport Dondinho played is known as football. Every language has its own word for it. In Brazil, where the national language is Portuguese, the word for the sport is *futebol*. In Spanish, it is *fútbol*. Germans call it *fussball*. Italians use the word *calcio*, while in Danish it's *fodbold*.

In the United States, the sport was once called *association football* so that it would not be confused with the other game that Americans call *football*. "Assoc." is short for association. From that comes the word *soccer*.

Every boy in Edson's neighborhood played soccer. He spent many hours playing with his friends. He was fast, and even though he was small for his age, he was one of the best.

The boys were too poor to buy a ball. So they got an old sock, stuffed it tightly with rags, and tied it up with string. This lumpy ball was kicked all around the streets in their neighborhood.

The goalposts might be a pair of old shoes. There were no real fields and very few organized leagues for children.

Edson did have one advantage: his father. Dondinho loved showing his boys all that he knew of the game he loved. They practiced dribbling and passing with the sock ball. He told them about the positions on the field and how to shoot the ball at the goal. He showed his sons how important it was to be able to play well with both feet, and how to control the ball no matter how it came to you. Edson loved this time with his father. The more Edson played, the more he had dreams of being a pro player like Dondinho. "One day," he told his friends, "I'm going to be as good as my dad."

About a year after they moved to Bauru, Dondinho finally got his second job. He worked at a government health clinic, sweeping floors and

helping the staff. Edson sometimes helped his father at work. Dondinho would use the time to tell Edson stories of his life in soccer. As Edson's dreams grew bigger, he grew even closer with his father.

Now that the family had enough money, Edson could finally go to school. Poor families in Brazil needed to save money for school fees and supplies before their children could begin classes. His mother and his aunt sewed up his old shorts and made him a nice shirt. He got a box of colored pencils to use in school.

But Edson, the boy who loved playing soccer, did not enjoy school. He did not like sitting still and he did not like doing homework. He often sneaked out to go swimming or to play soccer with his friends. When he was in class, he talked too much. As a punishment, his teacher sometimes stuffed his cheeks with paper! Other times, she made him kneel on hard, dry beans.

When Edson was about nine, the boys he played soccer with started calling him "Pelé." Most nicknames in Brazil are based on a person's name, what they look like, or how they act. But no one really knows what Pelé means. "I've been back to Bauru many times," Pelé later wrote, "and have asked all my old friends from those days, but they don't have a clue how or when it started."

At first, he hated the nickname. He was even suspended from school for hitting a boy who called him Pelé! But he eventually grew to love the name that he would soon make world famous.

CHAPTER 2
September 7 Team

Pelé and his friends watched the Bauru professional team and read stories of their soccer heroes around Brazil. When he was ten, Pelé and his friends formed a team of their own. They named it September 7, after the day Brazil gained independence from Portugal in 1822. It was also the name of a nearby street. But team September 7 wanted to do more than just play in the streets.

The first thing they needed was a real soccer ball. Pelé had the idea to collect stickers that pictured famous Brazilian soccer players. The stickers were sold with candy and other products.

If they saved enough stickers, they could earn a ball. Finding all the stickers was hard work, but finally the boys had all the stickers they needed. The team got their new soccer ball! Since collecting stickers was Pelé's idea, the ball stayed at his house and he became the team's unofficial captain.

Being the "keeper of the ball" did have some downsides. Whenever the team broke a window while they were playing, the neighbors went to Pelé's house to complain. And sometimes the boys would hit a light pole and knock out the electricity for a short while . . . and then everyone pointed at Pelé!

But stickers couldn't get them everything they wanted. The team also needed money for shirts and matching socks. And they still did not have soccer cleats. So they decided to change their team name to the Shoeless Ones.

One summer, the town held a youth soccer tournament. Pelé and his teammates wanted to enter, but the rules said that all players had to have soccer shoes. So the father of three of the players bought all the boys new cleats. Shoeless no more,

they had to change their name once again and became Amériquinha (say: ah-MARE-uh-KEEN-ya), which means "Little America" in English.

Though many of the other teams in the tournament had older players, Amériquinha won game after game. They reached the final match, which was played at the same stadium in Bauru where Dondinho played. A large crowd chanted Pelé's name as he scored a big goal, and Amériquinha went home with the championship.

After the game, Pelé was thrilled when his father said, "You played a beautiful game. I couldn't have played any better myself!"

Pelé's success in this tournament led the Bauru junior team to invite him to play with them. Dondinho was thrilled. But Celeste was not! Pelé's mother wanted him to focus on school and not follow the difficult life of a soccer player. But Pelé knew this was a big step toward his dream, so when he was just thirteen, he became a pro player, receiving a small payment for each game.

On the junior team, known as Baquinho (say: bah-KEEN-oh), he worked with a great coach named Waldemar de Brito. De Brito had played for Brazil's national team in the 1930s and 1940s. It was a great honor for this squad of young teenagers to have such a famous coach. "Baquinho

Waldemar de Brito

was a strong team," Pelé later wrote, "and under Waldemar we became even stronger. We were invincible." He meant that his team could not be stopped.

Led by Pelé's goal-scoring skill, Baquinho won a youth championship for the state of São Paulo in early 1955. In one game, he scored seven goals! Before the game, the stadium doorman almost didn't let him inside. He thought the pint-size Pelé was just a kid trying to sneak in without a ticket!

Meanwhile, Pelé still struggled with homework and with paying attention. He had to repeat one grade twice! But he managed to make it through and finish grade school when he was fifteen. It had taken him six long years to finish four years of school! His mother was still not pleased with all his soccer playing. She was very afraid that her

son would suffer an injury like Dondinho had.

As Pelé began playing more and more games, one person was missing from the stands: his mother. In fact, Celeste was so afraid he would be hurt, she never saw him play in person throughout his long, amazing career.

Pelé continued to show his skills in every game. He was able to keep the ball on his feet even as he ran at top speed. Though he was small, he could jump high and did very well at headers— bouncing the ball off his head as a pass or to take a shot at the goal. From de Brito, he learned the famous bicycle kick. In this move, Pelé turned his back to the goal and kicked his legs in the air one at a time. With the second leg, he kicked the ball from above his head toward the goal behind him! It is an amazing shot!

As Pelé developed his skills, his love for the game only continued to grow. It was more important to him than anything except his family.

When he played, he demonstrated that love and his tremendous spirit, and the fans responded with cheers!

The money he earned playing for Bauru was not very much. Pelé wanted to continue to help his family. He was too old for shining shoes, so Pelé got a job selling small meat pies to passengers on the many trains that stopped at Bauru station. He also worked for a while in a shoe factory.

At one point, a team in the city of Rio de Janeiro—then the capital of Brazil—invited Pelé

to come play for them. For Celeste, that was too much. She felt that Pelé was still just "a baby" and that Rio was too far away and too dangerous for a teenager. So Pelé stayed in Bauru . . . but he wondered for how much longer.

CHAPTER 3
Young Star

Waldemar de Brito continued to teach Pelé and other young players about the game they loved. But in early 1955, de Brito got an offer to move to the city of Santos in the state of São Paulo to work for another club. De Brito sat down with Dondinho and Celeste and told them that he thought Pelé should play for his new club, called

Santos Futebol Clube (or Santos FC). Celeste was still worried about her "baby." Dondinho trusted de Brito, however, São Paulo was not as big or as far away as Rio de Janeiro. It was only around two hundred miles from Bauru. Pelé, of course, was thrilled. Together, the family decided that the teenage star should take the next step in his career.

For the train ride to São Paulo, Celeste made Pelé his first pair of long pants. Dondinho traveled to São Paulo with Pelé.

Waldemar de Brito met them at the train station. Together, the trio headed to the Santos stadium, called Vila Belmiro. On the way, Pelé saw the tall skyscrapers of the city and marveled at the crowds of people. Once, a teacher had told Pelé that the ocean was salty. Now he had a chance to see for himself. He asked to stop at a São Paulo beach so he could taste the ocean to make sure.

"You can't imagine how grand it all was for me," he wrote later.

At the stadium, Pelé watched the team in action and then met the players—all older than he was. Many knew Dondinho from his long years as a player. One of them was Vasconselos, the team's star. "Put your mind at rest. He'll be safe with us," he told his old friend. Dondinho returned to Celeste knowing that his son was in good hands.

Pelé was very nervous. He was given a small room in a dormitory for single players. It was the first time Pelé had lived apart from his family, and he was sad. He was also worried about whether he could play with the older, bigger players on the Santos team. He couldn't even call his mother, since the family did not have a telephone back in Bauru.

"I was only fifteen, and suddenly I had to live with strange people in a strange place," he wrote later. "I was afraid of failing, but even more, I was afraid of the dark!"

After missing a penalty shot during a game, Pelé tried to sneak back home to Bauru. He was homesick. He had lost his confidence. He was also afraid he would never grow big enough to play with the larger players. As he tried to sneak out of the stadium unnoticed, the team assistant, Big Sabu, stopped him and convinced Pelé to give it one more shot. Sabu did not want Pelé to give up so easily. He told the teenager, "If you try running away again, I'll take that suitcase away from you!"

To get over his sadness, Pelé played harder than he ever had before. He practiced with the top Santos players and took part in some games with the junior team. The coaches told him that he had to gain weight and strength, so he ate more and more. The older players liked his energy,

on and off the field. It briefly earned him another nickname—Gasolina! They may have felt that Pelé's energy made the team run!

The Santos coaches knew how special their young player was. In the summer of 1956, Pelé got his first chance to play in a practice game with the senior team. Santos won, 6–1, and Pelé scored four goals!

Soccer Teams: Club and Country

Original World Cup trophy

Around the world, pro soccer players can play for two different kinds of teams. Their main team is the professional club that pays them. An athlete can play for a club in any country. A player from Brazil, for example, can play in a pro league in Italy, Spain, Mexico, or elsewhere. There are dozens or hundreds of professional soccer clubs in some countries.

The very best players can also take part in games with their country's national team. Each country has just one national team. Players are selected for this honor and then leave their pro clubs briefly to play for their national team.

National teams take part in tournaments, such as for the championship of a continent, or in the World Cup, which is played every four years. They also play one another in "friendlies," which are practice games that are not part of a tournament.

Later that year, on September 7, a familiar date to Pelé, he scored his first goal for Santos in an official league game. Because Pelé's family still did not have a phone, it took a whole day for this big news to make it back to Bauru!

Pelé continued splitting time with the junior and senior teams. Then the Santos star forward Vasconselos broke his leg. Pelé replaced him as a regular member of the senior team in early 1957.

Not long after, Pelé played his first game in the famous Maracanã Stadium in Rio de Janeiro and scored a hat trick—a term that describes when a player scores three goals in a single game.

He was the youngest player—at only seventeen—in the league and one of the top scorers. The little boy who kicked around a sock ball had become a superstar! By now, Pelé

Team Santos, 1957

had signed a new contract with Santos that paid him more than ever. He sent most of the money home. Dondinho used it to buy a small house so the family would have more room.

The family would no longer have to pay rent. Over the next two seasons, Pelé became a key part of the Santos team, playing around the state of São Paulo and traveling to other parts of Brazil.

By 1958, all of Brazil was looking forward to the World Cup, the international championship of soccer. Fans read soccer updates in newspapers and listened to the games on the radio. Those who

could afford tickets watched the club teams play live. It was the biggest story in the country, and millions awaited the news: Which players would be chosen for Brazil's national team?

After a tryout camp, the coaches called all the players together. They read off a list of the players on the World Cup team. Pelé was one of them!

CHAPTER 4
World Cup Glory

The 1958 World Cup was held in Sweden. That's a long way from Brazil! It would be Pelé's first trip on an airplane. In Brazil's final warm-up game, Pelé had hurt his knee. So he spent part of the long flight to Europe holding ice on it.

Sweden was thrilling for Pelé. He loved meeting new people and seeing the sights of Sweden's cities.

Some of the Swedish fans were very interested to see such a dark-skinned person as Pelé. Back home in Brazil, there were many mixed races of people within a country of varied cultures. Pelé felt lucky to have grown up in Brazil, where his African heritage was not so unusual. The people of Sweden, and much of Europe, however, were mostly white. They were very curious and excited to meet the Brazilian team, especially Pelé.

At the World Cup, Pelé had to miss Brazil's first two games as his knee continued to heal. He was finally in the starting lineup as a center forward for a game against the Soviet Union. He stood on the field with his teammates, his yellow jersey bright in the sunlight. A band played Brazil's national anthem. He felt a surge of love for his country. "When the band [plays that song], all of us Brazilians feel a strange force within us. . . . All of us [were] living in a dream, but none more so than me." Pelé did not score, but he made many key plays, and Brazil won, 2–0. They were one of only eight teams left in the tournament.

In their next game, against Wales, Pelé scored his first World Cup goal, and it was a beauty. He caught a long pass with his chest. As the ball fell to the ground, he spun and poked it with his toe into the back of the net. It was the game's only goal, putting Brazil into the semifinals.

The World Cup

Every four years, the top national teams play in the World Cup tournament. Hundreds of games are played in the years leading up to each World Cup, to determine which countries will make the tournament. The top thirty-two national teams play in the final, which is held in a different country each time. Billions of people around the world tune in to watch the games on TV.

The World Cup is run by the International Federation of Football, called FIFA (say: FEE-fah), which stands for the Fédération Internationale de Football Association, its name in French.

The first World Cup was held in 1930 in Uruguay. Only eight nations have ever won the World Cup:

Brazil (five wins)

Germany, Italy (four wins each)

Argentina, Uruguay (two wins each)

Spain, England, France (one win each)

(The World Cup was not held during World War II.)

Playing against France, Pelé was unstoppable. He scored three goals in the second half! The first two were from close to the goal, but the third was a twenty-yard blast. Brazil's 5–2 victory put them into the World Cup final in the city of Stockholm against the host nation, Sweden.

Sweden made its home fans happy—and shocked Brazil—by scoring just four minutes into the championship game. It was the first time Brazil had been behind in the whole tournament. But they quickly rallied. Pelé's teammates scored two goals for Brazil.

In the second half, Pelé scored to make it 3–1. It was one of the most remarkable goals of his career. Just as he had against Wales, he bounced a long pass off his chest. As the ball fell toward the ground, he flicked it over the head of the defender guarding him. Pelé sprinted past the

defender and kicked the ball into the goal before it hit the ground! The Swedish players could only stand and stare.

Pelé added another goal later, bouncing the ball off his head up and over the Swedish goalkeeper.

Not long after his second goal, the referee blew his whistle. The game was over. Brazil 5, Sweden 2. Brazil was the world champion!

Pelé was in tears as his teammates lifted him up on their shoulders. He was not afraid to show the great emotion of the moment. "The tears continued to flow, leaving trails in the sweat that still covered our faces," he later wrote.

The team received the World Cup trophy and met Sweden's King Gustav, all the while hearing the cheers of Brazil's fans in the stands.

When he returned to Brazil, Pelé and the national team were greeted as heroes. There were parades in Rio de Janeiro and São Paulo. After more than a week of celebrations, he finally made it back to Bauru, where another parade and his family awaited him.

The young man from Bauru was only seventeen years old and a world champion. Just a few years earlier, he had been playing without shoes on the dirt streets of Bauru. The most legendary career in soccer history was off to a flying start.

Soccer Positions

Most soccer teams have four main positions, but the eleven players on each team can be arranged in many different formations.

At the back is the goalkeeper. He is the only player who can use his hands, but only inside an area extending eighteen yards out from the goal. In front of him stand the defenders, which include fullbacks, sweepers, and center backs. Midfielders are in the middle and play both offense and defense. At the very front are

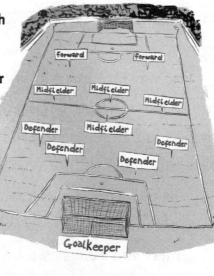

the forwards, who do most of the scoring.

CHAPTER 5
A Busy Time

In the fall of 1958, Pelé was already well-known to soccer fans around the world. But he still had his club job with the Santos team. Earlier that year, he had moved out of the dormitory and was living with a local family. On an off day, he and some teammates went to watch a girls' basketball game.

Pelé was interested in one of the players, and he asked to meet her. Rosemeri Cholbi was only fourteen, however, and Pelé was seventeen so they did not date right away. Rosemeri and Pelé saw a lot of each other with friends.

Rosemeri Cholbi

The only problem was that Rosemeri did not like soccer at all!

After he turned eighteen, Pelé served in the army for one year. In Brazil, there were no exceptions to this rule, even for national heroes! Every healthy man over eighteen had to complete his service. Pelé was stationed right in Santos and was treated like any other soldier. He had to learn how to march, how to clean the barracks, and

how to shoot a rifle. However, his service didn't keep him from playing soccer. Pelé played for an army team, for Santos, and for Brazil. During his year in the army, he played more than a hundred games!

After his army time was up, the Santos Club wanted to make the most of Pelé and their other famous Brazilian stars. The next couple of seasons were filled with endless matches. The club scheduled games around the world, sometimes making the athletes play even when they were very tired. "It was a brutal schedule," Pelé said later, "designed to make the Santos Club rich, and with small regard for the players." Although he was the team's most famous player, professional teams paid very little. And players had to follow all the rules or lose their jobs.

But the hectic schedule of matches led Pelé all over the world. Santos traveled to Central America and other parts of South America, and made a long trip to Europe. In Italy, Pelé and the team met Pope John XXIII. This was a big honor for Pelé, a lifelong Catholic. The team traveled to Egypt, where Pelé got to ride a camel. Wherever Pelé went, fans packed the stadiums to see his soccer magic. He welcomed them all with his big smile. Even when he was tired or sore, he wanted to make his fans happy.

Santos continued in Brazil's league play, winning the championship in 1961 and for the next four years. Santos also won the Intercontinental Cup in 1962, a tournament played among the world's best professional clubs. Pelé scored three goals in that championship game over a team from Portugal.

By this time, Pelé was beloved throughout Brazil. Fans couldn't wait to see what amazing skills he would show off next. He was also sought after by every club in the world. A team from Italy offered him half a million dollars to play there! He was twenty-one years old and that was ten times more than he was making at Santos!

The president of Brazil stepped in. He ruled that Pelé was a "national treasure." It would be illegal for him to play for any club outside Brazil. Such an honor had never been given to any player anywhere. Although Pelé probably earned less because of it, he was a proud Brazilian and followed the new law. Pelé was now *O Rei* . . . the King!

In the spring of 1962, Pelé injured his leg in a Santos game. Unfortunately, his injury came at a bad time, just as Brazil gathered its best players to defend their World Cup title. Pelé worked hard to get better. He played in the team's first game against Mexico and scored a goal.

But in their second game, against Czechoslovakia, he reinjured his leg and had to come out of the game. The team made it to the final match, but Pelé could not play. Pelé watched with mixed emotions from the sidelines as his beloved Brazilians won their second straight World Cup.

CHAPTER 6
The World of Pelé

After the injured muscle in his leg finally healed, Pelé returned to his high-scoring ways. Santos won several championships, including one among all the clubs in South America.

In 1965, Pelé finally asked Rosemeri's parents if he could marry her. Though he was used to playing in front of thousands of people, Pelé was nervous. He went fishing for a day with Rosemeri's father. Pelé asked if he could marry

Rosemeri. The two men continued to fish but her father never gave Pelé an answer. After a long day on the water, he told Pelé, "We'll see." Finally, after they had met with Rosemeri's mother, the marriage was approved!

Pelé and Rosemeri were married by a priest at his parents' house in 1966. Because he was so famous, Pelé's fans had filled the streets outside, hoping to see the couple. They could not leave the house for hours!

For their honeymoon, Pelé and Rosemeri toured Europe. They went to France, Switzerland, Germany, Austria, and Italy. In Rome, he got the chance to introduce Rosemeri to Pope Paul VI.

When they returned to Brazil, it was time to get ready for the 1966 World Cup. And the other teams heading to England for the matches were ready to take on Brazil. In games against both Bulgaria and Portugal, the opposing players knew that they had to defeat Pelé to win their matches

against the Brazilian team. And so, again and again, players fouled Pelé, kicking him in the legs. The other athletes' shameful behavior injured Pelé's body and also his pride. He no longer wanted to play for his national team. Portugal won their third game, and Brazil was out of the World Cup!

In 1967, Pelé had a very busy year! After Rosemeri gave birth to Kelly Cristina, their first child, Pelé visited the United States with Santos.

His appearances there set records for the biggest crowds up to that time in US soccer history. Even in a nation where soccer was not that popular, Pelé was well-known. Later in the year, he visited

Africa, including stops in Senegal, Nigeria, and Congo. He was mobbed everywhere he went. "To these people, who had little possibility of ever escaping the crushing poverty in which they found themselves, I somehow represented a ray of hope," he wrote later.

In 1969, the Santos team was on another tour of Africa. The people of the Nigerian state of Biafra were at war with each other. However, people on both sides of the fighting wanted to see Pelé play. For two days the fighting stopped.

Pelé and Santos played, and the war resumed once they had left Nigeria. This single event showed just how big an international star Pelé really was.

Meanwhile, reporters in Brazil had been keeping careful track of Pelé's scoring. They determined that he had scored nearly a thousand goals during his professional career. A countdown began. Finally, on November 19, 1969, he scored on a penalty kick to reach the magic number.

Fans poured onto the field and lifted him high on
their shoulders. Photographers crowded around
him. His jersey was pulled off and a new one put
on. Instead of a shirt bearing his famous number
10, the new jersey read "1000." Only a very few
players had ever scored that many goals, and none
had been as famous as Pelé.

Even as fans showed their love for him, Pelé returned it. In a speech to the crowd, he thanked them for their support. He also urged them to help the young people of Brazil who were living in poverty. Pelé never forgot that his own youth had not been easy.

CHAPTER 7
One More Championship

As the 1970 World Cup approached, Pelé reconsidered playing for Brazil. The poor sportsmanship of the last Cup tournament had concerned him. But if Pelé played for his national team now, he would become one of a handful of players ever to take part in four World Cups.

By this time, even more people than usual were able to watch Pelé. This was the first World Cup to be broadcast live in color on TV. More than a billion people were now watching the greatest player ever! Some had only read about him or seen grainy black-and-white highlights. In front of this huge audience, Pelé and Brazil put on an amazing show of soccer.

Pelé scored a goal in the team's first game, a win

over Czechoslovakia. He then made a pass that led to the only goal in Brazil's 1–0 win over England. Victories over Peru, Romania, and Uruguay sent Brazil to the final game against Italy.

Early in that game, Pelé rose above a defender to hit the ball with his head. Pelé smacked the ball off his forehead and into the goal. As he had done more than one thousand times before, he raced around the field, celebrating with his teammates.

The pictures of that celebration in Mexico were now being shared around the world.

The celebration continued after Brazil won the game and their third World Cup, beating Italy 4–1. Once again, Pelé's teammates and some fans carried him off the field on their shoulders.

Before the big party that night, Pelé went back to the dressing room. He took time to pray and thank God for all that had happened. Once back in Brazil, the team enjoyed more parades and parties. Finally, Pelé left the celebrations behind. He wanted to be back in Santos with Rosemeri, who was pregnant. In August, their son, Edson, was born. But everyone called him by his nickname: Edinho.

After the 1970 World Cup, Pelé wanted to go back and finish high school. He wanted to eventually go to college. As he traveled more and more, he realized how important education was. He wanted to set an example for his children. But to earn a spot at a university, he had to pass some tough tests. He worked with teachers and studied hard.

Pelé was accepted at the University of Santos in the fall of 1970. Over the next three years, he took classes in between playing games for Santos and earned a degree in physical education.

During this time, he decided to stop playing for Brazil's national team for good. After a game on July 18, 1971, he took off his bright yellow jersey for the final time. He ran a lap around the field to thank the 180,000 people who had packed the stadium.

In his final years with Santos, he made sure to use his fame to help other players. For many years, pro soccer players in Brazil were not paid anything near what they deserved. They were also not protected as other workers were. If a player was injured, some teams would not even pay their medical bills. Pelé and other star players met with government officials to try to correct this. They didn't get very far, and it would be years before the situation improved.

Pelé also got a chance to teach soccer to children. He signed a deal with Pepsi that created a worldwide series of soccer clinics. Pelé planned the lessons and even worked at some of the clinics.

He also recorded a video with his good friend Santos coach Julio Mazzei that showed young people how to improve their soccer skills.

And then Pelé wrapped up his long career with the Santos team. In a game on October 2, 1974, he suddenly grabbed the ball with his hands.

He ran with it to the center circle of the field and knelt down with his hands in the air. This was a signal to everyone in the stadium that he was leaving the field—and the sport—for good.

It took a moment for everyone to realize what Pelé meant, but then they understood. "The crowd realized what I was doing," he wrote later. "I was honoring them for the years they had honored me."

And that was it. As the crowd cheered and his teammates and opponents clapped, Pelé walked slowly off the field for the final time in Brazil.

With the Santos and Brazil teams, Pelé had already conquered most of the world of soccer. He was the only three-time World Cup champion and was among the leading goal-scorers of all time. He was a Brazilian national treasure and a hero to billions of fans around the world. But he had his eye on a new goal: the United States.

CHAPTER 8
Pelé's Triumphs Continue

During the entire span of Pelé's career in Brazil, soccer had not been very popular in the United States. Some immigrant Americans followed the teams from their native countries. But even though there was a national team, very few Americans played. In 1968, a new professional league was formed, hoping to bring "the world's sport" to the United States. The North American Soccer League (NASL) wanted to attract attention, so it recruited soccer stars from around the world.

In 1975, after he left Santos, Pelé was asked to join the New York Cosmos. He was thirty-four years old and his best playing days were behind him. But he still loved the game, and he was willing to try something new. And the Cosmos understood that world-famous Pelé could attract new fans to the sport.

But first, Brazil had to let him go! US secretary of state Henry Kissinger, a soccer fan, persuaded Brazil's president to allow Pelé, the "national treasure," to play in the United States. The Cosmos gave Pelé a contract that paid him almost

 four times more than the highest-paid American baseball player at the time. It was more money than Pelé had earned in all his years with Santos combined—more than $4 million!

The great star arrived to a mixed reaction. Soccer fans were thrilled. Many American sportswriters, however, didn't understand all the fuss. *How could you love a sport where you can't use*

your hands? they joked. Surprisingly, the Cosmos' early games with Pelé were not sellouts, and the team lost more games than it won. It had been a huge risk for the Cosmos to bring Pelé to New York.

By 1977, however, the gamble had paid off. The Cosmos had become a huge hit everywhere they played. The games were all televised. Huge crowds packed stadiums across the country. Other great stars joined Pelé on the team, including Germany's Franz Beckenbauer and Italy's Giorgio Chinaglia. During Pelé's third season, the Cosmos won the Soccer Bowl, the NASL championship game.

When Pelé decided to end his career in America, a special farewell match was held at Giants Stadium in New Jersey. On October 1, 1977, the Cosmos arranged a game against Santos,

Pelé's old club from Brazil. The biggest crowd in American soccer history up to that time (75,616) filled every seat. In the first half, Pelé played for the Cosmos and scored a goal. In the second half, he switched sides and played one more time for Santos. He ended his career with a total of 1,281 goals. He was thirty-six years old.

Before the game, Pelé spoke to the fans. He thanked them for supporting him. Then he called on the people in the stands to repeat one word, over and over. Expressing his feelings for his fans, for the game, and for people everywhere, he called out, "Love! Love! Love!" The fans roared back all the "Love" to Pelé!

At halftime, he gave his Cosmos jersey to Dondinho to thank him for getting him started in soccer, and he hugged Rosemeri. After the game, the players from both teams carried Pelé off the field for the final time.

American Soccer

Soccer has been played in America since the 1860s. Only recently, however, has it become widely popular.

Although the American Youth Soccer Organization (AYSO) had begun in 1964, there was no successful professional soccer league in the United States until the North American Soccer League (NASL) began in 1968. Pelé and the New York Cosmos kick-started a soccer boom during his years in the United States, from 1975 to 1977.

In 1994, the United States hosted its first World Cup in nine different cities.

Major League Soccer (MLS), which began in 1996, has more than twenty teams playing in the United States and Canada.

After retiring from playing, Pelé chose to work with several businesses in Brazil and spend time with his children. Rosemeri had given birth to their daughter Jennifer, their third child, in 1978.

As always, Pelé tried to help children and others. He continued to travel and to hold soccer clinics that were sponsored by Pepsi. He made sure to meet as many children as he could. As one of the most famous people in the world, he was greeted by presidents and royalty wherever he went.

In 1994, he was named a worldwide goodwill ambassador for the United Nations Educational, Scientific and Cultural Organization. He was fifty-four years old.

In 1995, he was named Minister of Sport for the government of Brazil. He took advantage of this job to once again make life better for Brazil's soccer players. By 1998, he had created rules that made soccer clubs treat their players more fairly. The government passed the "Pelé Law," which helped free players to change teams, provided insurance for their injuries, and encouraged owners to pay them more.

Pelé's family continued to grow. He had divorced Rosemeri over ten years earlier, and in 1994, he married Assíria Lemos. Pelé and Assíria had twins, Joshua and Celeste, two years later.

At the end of the twentieth century, votes were taken around the world to name the best soccer player of the century. Pelé was the winner in nearly all of them! The world organization for soccer, FIFA, named him one of two Players of the Century, too.

Pelé divorced Assíria in 2008 and married Marcia Aoki in 2016. He continues to act as a spokesman for companies that are interested in having one of the most famous athletes in the world represent their businesses. He also helps raise money for charities, including UNICEF and a children's hospital in Brazil. He still meets with children around the world to encourage them to play soccer.

Pelé has dazzled fans with his amazing soccer skills for decades. He remains an international superstar and the greatest soccer player in the world. He has become a symbol for the game of soccer itself.

Pelé is simply the best!

Timeline of Pelé's Life

1940 — Born in the village of Três Corações, Brazil

1955 — Joins pro club Santos FC in São Paulo

1958 — Wins World Cup with Brazilian national team

1966 — Marries Rosemeri Cholbi

1967 — Daughter Kelly is born

1969 — Scores 1,000th career goal

1970 — Wins third World Cup with Brazilian national team; becomes first player to win three World Cups

— Son Edinho is born

1974 — Retires from Santos FC

1975 — Plays for New York Cosmos of North American Soccer League (NASL)

1977 — Leads Cosmos to NASL Soccer Bowl championship

— Plays final game as a professional, for the New York Cosmos against Santos in the first half and for Santos against the Cosmos in the second

1978 — Daughter Jennifer is born

1994 — Marries Assíria Lemos

1995 — Becomes Brazil's Minister of Sport

1996 — Twins Joshua and Celeste are born

2000 — Named one of two players of the century by FIFA

2016 — Marries Marcia Aoki

Timeline of the World

1939 — World War II begins in Europe

1945 — The United Nations is founded

1949 — China is taken over by communists led by Mao Tse-tung

1954 — British runner Roger Bannister becomes the first person to run a mile in under four minutes

1957 — The Soviet Union puts the first man-made satellite in orbit

1960 — A new city called Brasília becomes the capital of Brazil

1964 — The Beatles play their first concert in the United States

— The United States signs the Civil Rights Act into law

1969 — Apollo 11 lands the first men on the moon

1971 — The first e-mail is sent

1976 — America celebrates its bicentennial, its two hundredth birthday

1989 — The Berlin Wall falls, ending separation of East and West Germany

1991 — The first public website is posted

1994 — Nelson Mandela becomes the first black president of South Africa

2008 — Barack Obama becomes the first African American to be elected US president

Bibliography

*Books for young readers

*Buckley, James Jr. *Pelé: A Photographic Story of a Life.*
New York: DK Publishing, 2007.

*Cline-Ransome, Lesa. *Young Pelé: Soccer's First Star.* New York:
Random House, 2007.

Harris, Harry. *Pelé: His Life and Times.* New York: Welcome Rain
Publishers, 2002.

Pelé, with Robert L. Fish. *Pelé: My Life and the Beautiful Game.*
New York: Doubleday, 1977.

Pelé, with Orlando Duarte and Alex Bellos. *Pelé:
The Autobiography.* New York: Simon & Schuster, 2006.

*Pelé, with Frank Morrison. *For the Love of Soccer.* New York:
Disney-Hyperion, 2010.